To All Appearances

University of Illinois Press *Urbana Chicago London*

Josephine Miles

To All Appearances

Poems New and Selected

Acknowledgment is made to publishers of earlier books from which some of these poems were selected: from *Lines at Intersection,* Macmillan Company, 1939; from *Poems on Several Occasions,* New Directions, 1941; and from *Local Measures,* Reynal and Hitchcock, 1946.

The poems from *Kinds of Affection,* copyright 1962, 1963, 1964, 1965, 1966, 1967, are reprinted with the permission of Wesleyan University Press. Seven of those poems first appeared in *Poetry:* "Love at a distance can mean," "The doctor who sits at the bedside of a rat," "I walked along the river path, the river," "Still early morning, the wind's edge," "Does the world look like a park to you? Yes, almost suddenly," "Down from another planet they have settled to mend," and "Apart from branches in courtyards and small stones."

The poems from *Prefabrications,* 1956, and *Poems 1930–1960,* 1960, are reprinted with the permission of Indiana University Press.

Some of the previously uncollected poems have appeared in *American Poems, Café Solo, Goat's Head, Hyperion, The Nation, New Mexico, The New Yorker, Poetry Now, Southern Review, Street Poems,* and *Voyages.* "Poetry South," "Circus," and "Identity" appeared in *Civil Poems,* Oyez, 1966, and "Fields" and "Paths" in *Fields of Learning,* Oyez, 1968.

Library of Congress Cataloging in Publication Data

Miles, Josephine, 1911–
To all appearances.

I. Title.
PS3525.I4835T6 811'.5'2 74-9000
ISBN 0-252-00439-6
ISBN 0-252-00443-4 (pbk.)

Contents

Poems New

and Selected

from *Lines at Intersection*

from *Poems on Several Occasions*

from *Local Measures*

from *Prefabrications*

Poems New

Solstice

Resting slow and extreme, our sun produces
Bauble on bauble
Plumcolored and apple
To say
Bear with me.
In tissue paper packages, small actions of sunlight
Glisten, and I begin to proceed
Right now
Out of these toyshops of expectation
Through accountancies of equinox, into
Full summer:
My radiant radical liberal reactionary revolutionary conservative
Plan.

Thread

Take an emotion, how can it be?
          I cannot do crochet
                    But take a doily—
The white threads in and out
In, say, a shell,
                    Loop and lock
                    Filling out this doily.
It would protect a curved back of a chair velour
From a neck velour.

Now the emotion: where the white thread
                    Should continue itself into its measurement,
                    Doily of heart diffidently skips
                    Becomes a repeat of pearls or this or that
                    A purple thread as of the outset purple.
You crazy feeling
                    Let the hard line bask
                    On simple pattern, not your prying
                    Arabesques of what? flesh? water-color?

How I Caught Up in My Reading

After the season was summer
And students were rocked in their summer cradles,
I began to catch up.
First I read many accumulated magazines
On the president's unemployment commission, for example,
And revelations about Senator Dodd.
Wasn't he dead?
Then I read
A number of old novels like *Anna Karenina*
And a number of new science fictions,
Then I read
Your thesis and Betty's thesis and Clinton's
Thesis
And advised alterations
In marginal notes of great thickness.
Then I read the Berkeley Daily Gazette and the recipes
In *Better Homes.* Then
I read a lot of poems, all the pamphlets in the house, hundreds piled up, friends and strangers, poems. And answered. And replied.
Then
I looked around
And read one poem
Again
Again.

Conservancies

Plums on the ground
Lay with a soft sound
And the sweet sense of dissolution they have.
She used to pick them up
With a scoop, thickened with bees.
She would carry away into bottles what she could save
And the cinnamon worked in the kitchen
Saying *save*.

Now when the lingering fresh breezes
Flurry in the field rows
Some sifts of clear summer air,
She pickles the puffs in clear jars,
Brings them out
In winter scarcity,
Gives everybody on his plate of melathion
A rich spoonful of air.

Tract

Old tract, the houses of wood-siding
Old callas at the drain pipes, a frontal
Cedar, line among lots
Cabs, a wagon, a pick-up
And the bay not far, a dozen miles over town.
A boy on a bike now and again
Makes up a tunafish sandwich and starts off.
Few go out otherwise, they stay in to listen.

For some tracts, a whole range
Of mountains takes the bay's place,
Holds all the answer or loss
Behind curtains as tears.
For some, beyond the outskirts of the houses,
More callas, more houses.

New Tract

Streets under trees
lamps in their windows
gathering dark,

Comfortable coming of home,
fussing and crying, tears of the tired, yet lamplit
windows under the trees
trees under opening stars.

Work done, car in the port,
children cleared and asleep under stars,
why not enough?

Held in the hold of the mountainous night
And the bend of the street,
why not enough?

Building and bearing
street after street in the town to the mountains and on,
state after state in trees of the plains with a plenty or spare

and by rivers
why not enough?

Later from night
trees upon street
droop of the dark sides, haggard of morning,
show that it was.

Playing

I pressed and stirred the envelope of cream
In my teacup, trusting it would melt and infuse,
Sweet cream, sweet cardboard.
While down the road the Chinese maestro chased
A boy amid his swarm of scores
Trusting he would catch up.

Hum, hum, the notes stang
And the hoop kept rolling.
All success, maestro! I join
Midconcert with the long sweep
Of bows to leftward, awkward, spoons
And fields run on, snapping their barbed scores.

Grey

The grey man,
Blood has flowed off out of him
River safe to sea.
By his bones, concepts viscous as honey, but grey.
He sits covered with a blanket, and he runs his chair
Down the hall of where this is.
Look deep into his sunbeam eye
The volunteers, toward whom he says
My job is to retrieve
Lost efficiencies in the Stock Paper Company.

Veins thick with magentas of memory
Carry me to my work.
Transfusion on the left drains away
The dirty heart,
Foot at right
Lifts off brake and gas pedal.
Custards and alpha tones
Encourage him to get into his shoes and go.

Visit

Cricket complained quite a bit how lights wept falling
In and out her wings
Stars in her eyes
Dimming.

Bear
Took the market approach
Up and down.
Brrr, said cricket.

In his strong voice
Bear talked all around her
Built the place she was in
Ordered up sweet rolls, had to go.

You take care now, bear said.
Bye, bye, son, said cricket.

If You Will

Shall I pull the curtains against the coming night?
No, there is still a fine sun in the tree tops; let them be.
All right; now it is darker; shall I now
Close out the dark? You will close out the light.
All right; how quick the dark comes. But see how the moon
Floods as it floods the earth even this room.
Moonlight, it's time to sleep, shall I draw now
Curtains against the cold? It's summer weather.
Shall I? Yes, if you will; the light will pass.
It is your life that stands beyond the glass.

Scape

A bad conscience silent and major
Gives a beard to
Cleaves a hoof of
Raises flames around
Its woolly lamb.

The lamb
Leaps from the pyre
Looks at the populace
Licks its cinders and
Cries like a kid.

How to Win a Soccer Match

When the players get down close to the goal, the ghost goalie
(He's a ghost goalie because there's no field there yet,
And he's playing on it, active sportsman)
Raises his rifle and sights along it;
By the rules of the game (ghost game) he's the only one
Who can use his hands.

Retrospective

Once I didn't think that much about making the bomb.
In the halls I turned
Away from the machinists who made it,
I said sorry
To Japanese friends, especially one from Hiroshima
I agreed with in liking Isaac Walton.
Not thinking of the dead as death makers,
I said doubly in my heart about nightfall
May there be peace again.

Then a quarter century of Chaucer went very fast,
Now in one way, by a foreshortened view and exaggerated,
I have lived to the time in this free city where I say,
Look what I have been doing,
I have been making the bomb, creating,
Letting be created, the following real people:
John Mitchell, General Westmoreland,
Sheriff Madigan, John Mitchell,
The list keeps sticking so it doesn't get to the big names.

Jump: is Nasser mine? And Ky mine?
Somebody asks a syllabus for the next quarter:
How to keep from making
John Mitchell, General Westmoreland.
Composition: to think again
To work again the slow used-over clay.

Witness

Gassed going between classes
Students said little,
Huddled their books and ran.
As helicopter crews waved down low at them
They were silent
Yelled and were silent.

Now the trees speak, not running or reading
But with cast leaves tallying
The cost of a gas deterrent.
My throat alive still cries
But how to tell without dying
Is not told by the dying trees.

My Fear in the Crowd

The thousand people stand in the sunlight,
They are taking in the messages of the speakers
Deliberately, they are weighing the judgments,
They are making up their minds.

The sun is on their shoulders, weight of the earth,
They know it, and they are not despairing.
Against odds, they may consider quietly and freely
What they will do.

Who knows then, not I
And I am desperate in no knowledge,
If later, somewhat dispersed, they will yell
And turn and burn the place where they stood.

But look, the May light
Outlines each shape, each moving
Out from the crowd, each carrying
In his own mind the place where he stood.

Vitamin

He comes forward out of his vitamin shell
Into his vitamin shell,
Sleek. Well, mom,
Where do we go from here?

Into the good life. But isn't that
Where we are at?
Into more of the same, son. There's the story,
Sinfjotli, Signi's son.

Even as love and honor breed and await him,
Bus him into love's slum, toward what he is not.
Groggy with vitamin D, the sunshine vitamin,
He is not privation, but its compatriot.

Chairman

Now the old men are getting nervous.
They are shedding so much blood not theirs
That they begin to taste it, and the acrimony
Colors their tongues.
In the board room
Freshly shaven
They vote, ten or eleven to seven
To kill.

They feel in their age a tenderness for the young,
So they set at the head of the table,
Blond to the grey at his left and his right, a charismatic
Youth, a lightfoot babe,
Early mellow
Who, nodding to left and to right,
Will move the previous question,
To kill, and to kill.

Views from Gettysburg

Students all, we sit on the ridge, in a Pontiac GTO.
The western hills are blue in the haze of noon,
The near woods dense and cool, a breath of wind
In the wheat rippling toward us,
Fences cutting
An angle at the peach orchard, very quiet.

One or two small boys off at a distance
Man a gun emplacement; up through the wheat
Toward them come in the smoke and flash of fire
The faces of the confederate dead, boys also.
They come right into the cannister shot,
They look up to us as they come in bunches, their flags
Surging and dropping.

Where is the vantage? Vantage from depth mistaken
Or height assumed?
Faces look up into deflective glass
Responseless, downward to a beveled screen,
Windshielded both. Where is the voice to answer?
Where the fair fight?

Northern General Meade, we are looking for you
In the suburbs. Now it is summer,
Sailboats in the lagoons slip gaily,
Bourbon barrels in arcades, brigades of houses
Come over costly ridges for the view.
General Meade holds position, not confused
By wrenched faces fighting as they come.

Back in town, as the clock strikes one,
A math professor takes up his math class,

And I am eating, for the first time,
A sweet sour mix of Pennsylvanian
Apples and hocks, hot as the day is.
Up from the valley
Keep coming white faces into volleys of thunder.

We are in some kind of fight for or against with the union army.
Tired and footsore in the GTO,
Ready for a quick look at the news and to bed,
We sit staring into open faces.
There they come again, kooks now,
Straight in the camera fire, rebel yells,
Expressions fixed and wild.

Lianas, ropes of jungles, death defying,
Caves, thatches, trapped pits, a guerrilla
Concept of fever, a white Ghanian
Hill bungalow beyond the plain
Grasses of Gettysburg. General Meade,
What is your command
As we look downward?

It's a clear view up here from the fourth story
Of a Telegraph Avenue apartment. When the crowds rise
Between the level bake shops and the drug store
Their white eyes are clear.
Where is the mace or free beer to stop them?
They are looking with horror to a height like this one.

Let me alone, do you hear,
I am whole and sound,
I will stay that way,
I am walking along
The road to Emmetsburg in the wrong direction.

Or, pile up my guts in my hand
And I will carry them
Up to the stone wall at its angle and over it
To silence just one cannon.
I speak into its mouth: Silence!
Most of the brigades go together
Suffer thirst, cheer. They pick up the banner and follow together.

Night in the Blue Ridge, Corrington's boys are returning
From their visit to the battlefield.
They are winding along those heights,
See nothing below them,
But the west is widening the white of its eye.

Traveling, or going on, or in pursuit,
A wheel will hit a bend in the western grade, and then below
Evening in the river trees, among clusters
Of roofs, and one spire
White in the twilight, ready as memory.
Many the tired night, late lamps, rays scattered
Over the leafy spire, husbanding light.

But how do I see past this bend again,
Southern fields
Wide and open, full fields, no town,
Where do I turn?

Over the shoulder, up at the hill crest
High in the late sun, the maple cluster
And the town cluster round its spire. Up there,
Head back, eyes lifted,
Tired I come to you, Is it home, I must ask, master,
Is it father, lord?

From the lectern angle, the lecturer
Waits, watching,
Ready to fire,
Holds till he sees
The whites of their eyes,
Then lets them have it—
Instruction, quick from the holster,
Low and steady,
At a little angle.
They take it well,
Heads toward writing fists
Ducked in deflection,
Bent elbows dispersing
Ninety-pound jolts of information
Over a wide radius.

I was a soldier not for money or office.
I was young, single, physically able,
And my country was assailed.
West and north of the Spangler House, on low ground
Pickett for Lee took up, according to G. R. Stewart, the tactic of Napoleon.
A direct rush under cast iron ball and shell,
Rending the limbs of oak trees.

A few hundred went forward under Armistead.
There she goes! The deep and steady roar.
The blue-bellies ran from the Angle and the flags went backward.
The ground was fairly jammed with Pickett's men.
In all positions, lying and kneeling.
Back from the edge were many standing and firing
Over those in front. Every foot of ground was occupied
By men engaged in mortal combat
In every position possible under arms.

There was a sudden swinging of clubbed muskets,
Not bayonets. Everything trembled in balance.
A general said, Will you see your colors storm the wall alone?
A general said, The best the men can do
Is to get out of this. Let them go.
Thrusts, yells, blows, shots, and undistinguishable conflict,
The strange resistless impulse moved them.

Throwing of stones: the local traprock weathers
Into chunks conveniently sized and shaped.
It takes half a minute to load a rifle,
So throwing stones is faster.
Where are the men who fought us, losses five to one?
A rooster must fight best on his own dunghill.
Did you see any Massachusetts or New York regiment
Come down and run over the 72nd?
I would like to meet the man who said it!

A man by the name of Metz, belonging to my company,
Fought his way back to it, and said,
I thought that if I were to get killed
I would like to be near somebody who knew me.
He fell across the stone wall, crossways.
Three o'clock.

From an apartment highrise or steep residential
Hill, the regiments
Of visible houses are implacable.
Contemplate one broken line
Multiplied, and there's no day for you.
Night has a different portion, then the stars
Astronomize a heaven to earth and give you
Peace from the other side of understanding.

So it is day, noon even, when the houses
Turn, take up their arms,
Flash in the gunsmoke fog
Signals to say they'll have the ridge by sundown.
Forty floors down, you see them looking toward you,
Marshaled
From coal beds far under peach orchards
Yelling what? It is hard to hear them.

Along the veins of coal a life is lived,
Half standing, lying,
Half breathing, smothering.
Black to the core and to the whites of eyes.
What are those lanterns glimmering?
The weight of wealth of earth sometimes lets up
To sleep at night, collapses others.
A steady craft, capable at five years,
Informs its pride.

An astronaut intensively informed
Reclines to head room
Along the veins of space, its folded brain.
Thinks, thinks in there,
Does calculations,
Comes out to walk, goes back to breathe,
Stifled among his rations. He is up and away.
And coal somewhere, even at that airless extremity,
Keeps him, gives him his life.

Softly the capitol hill surveys its scene,
The roads of its marble caverns
On which it governs,
Litter of tombs.

Each stone figure put to sitting
Upon his grave
Faces outward, skyward and sunward,
Thinking to live.

Underground, whoo, whoo, something is coming,
That's the ticket,
Straight up the aisle breaking the silence
Dirt flies out of the railway tunnel.

On the other side of the track and valley
Tracking his hole,
The old mole is busy upchucking
A new hill.

We will build up the hill and come up so the white of the eye
Will be lambent and clear
At our height and will look to us level
And straight as we near.

And the word will be *lawmaking*, made for us here as we stand
Not back home, not below, not down under,
But ready
And here at your hand.

Man himself
Taken aloof from his age and his country
And standing in the presence of Nature and of God
With his passions, his doubts, his rare prosperities,
And inconceivable wretchedness, is chief, if not sole,
Theme among these nations. Taken aloof.

Charles Neil, Kathy Caulfield, Kathy Csere,
Mary Lee Peyton, Gene Slear, and I, students all,
And Stephen Crane, George Stewart, James Dickey,
Ralph Ellison, Bill Corrington, De Toqueville, students all,
Have been riding around Little Big Round Top in the GTO,
Admiring the plenty of places to park.

But channel changes, windshield cracks, street feet
Get down to the ground
Walk over the plain ground,
To parley, in the presence of age and of country,
The chief and level theme
Of civil life.

Circus

It seems to me that a world of hurt
Pounds at my heart. I cannot care
If this is today's sickness or tomorrow's
Prospect of fear.

So I look at a circus.
Each performer moves to entertain
On elephant, bicycle, trapeze, and high wire,
With flexible, ardent, unsharable pain.

Identity

When the third son went out
To seek his fortune,
He sought his fortune, not himself.
He knew he was
The third son.

But what his fortune was,
In what journey,
City, cave, woodland, racetrack,
Air,
Needed moving toward.

Some, I have heard, stay home.
It is the first and second
Son. They ask, who am I?
Any answer they may get
Is premature.

Fortunes

Chills were hopping in my skin
As I asked for a cup of tea
And my friend gave me also
A bag of fortune cookies.

Not one, not a handful, but a bagful.
That kind of bliss
Which steams from a cup of tea
Steamed to me.

Every probable, every possible,
Every impossible
Fortune from here to Mishima.
It was the world.

I cracked the first cookie, and it said
Do not open more than one
Of these fortunes
At a time.

The American Flag

Betsy Ross is at work
On this star spangled morning.
Her needle threads
The striped skies.

What drear flannel from her looms?
Cut to exact size, it lines out stripes
And dry mustard to the tinge of dun.
What is she doing, old lady,
In the back of that Cad steering westward?
Pushing that diesel, gray caul bobbing
VW after VW?

Mobilized her cavalcade,
A yard wide
Carbonized wool,
Her tooth in it.

Poetry South

Snug in the cradle, we murmured Pre-Raphael
Greetings to Lochinvar,
With the first World War picked up sincerely
The Scott of the South and of Edward.

To this poem there was lineage
Clear following edge, many foldings
Of flesh or of satin, the easy extra
Anapests of the south.

Curve Rackham into the Pooh, curve
Benchley past Wylie Elinor, you are wrong
To think of Philip, curve Lardner
Past Cather or Cabell, a high school of south and of edward.

Then when the banks closed, many poets
Started singing Hanns Eisler at picnics
And got out on the harvesting, hiking, open road
Leaving their Saintsbury ailing in edward.

But south to the rescue, the gallant, the Southern
And Kenyon, swung by the rose vines to Empson and Kafka,
Suggesting a stay in that garden,
As real as another, and souther.

Confirmed by pre-Cromwell, by garlands
For Donne and for William
Yeats on his strand,
The line of resilience, of infinite doubt and decision,

The bookmen, the learners who bend in their towers
And flowers, set ever a finer
Point on the petal, draw ever a finer
Subjunctive from south and from edward.

And they give for a syllable, juncture,
Pause for a dactyl, atoning
The gap between person and person, phrasemaking,
Edward for edward.

But we see in the aisles of the street and the hall
The listeners, waiting to hear
Who is there. And we see on the roads
The traffic of travel, coming to share who is there.

Bursts north to the cities, to give us
A name for our Raphael, Stevens;
A name for our Lowell, like Lowell?
A nameless vocation of thousands, of Whitman in thousands,
Reclaiming the south.

Fields

When we go out into the fields of learning
We go by a rough route
Marked by colossal statues, Frankenstein's
Monsters, AMPAC and the 704,
AARDVARK, and deoxyribonucleic acid.
They guard the way.
Headless they nod, wink eyeless,
Thoughtless compute, not heartless,
For they figure us, they figure
Our next turning.
They are reading the book to be written.
As we start out
At first daylight into the fields, they are saying,
Starting out.

In every Sage leaf is contained a toad
Infinitely small.

Carbonized grains of wheat unearthed
From the seventh millennium B.C. town of Jarmo
In the Tigris Euphrates basin
Match the grains of three kinds of wheat still extant,
Two wild, one found only in cultivation.
The separate grains
Were parched and eaten,
Or soaked into gruel, yeasted, fermented.
Took to the idea of bread,
Ceres, while you were gone.
Wind whistles in the smoky thatch,
Oven browns its lifted loaf,
And in the spring the nourished seeds,
Hybrid with wild grass,
Easily open in a hundred days,
And seeded fruits compact and dry,

Store well together.
They make the straw for beds,
They ask the caring hand to sow, the resting foot
To stay, to court the seasons.

Basil: hatred: king over pain.

What did you do on the last day of day camp?
First we did games, running around and playing.
Then we did crafts, making things.
Then we did nature, what goes on and on.
Eventually a number
Of boys have got big enough
Through all the hazards of drag racing, theft, and probation,
To start for junior college, two transfers away,
Mysterious as Loch Ness.
While of grandmothers a number
Have stooping arrived to seventy or eighty
And wave the boys on, shaking
With more absent-minded merriment than they have mustered
In a half century.

King Henry the Eighth consumed many daisies
In an attempt to rid himself of ulcers.

Algebra written across a blackboard hurts
As a tight shoe hurts; it can't be walked in.
Music, a song score, hurts,
How far lies one note from another?
Graft hurts, its systems of exploitation
In cold continuance.
Argosies of design, fashions to which the keys
Rest restlessly in an Egyptian tomb.

In every Sage leaf is contained a toad
Infinitely small.

Paths

Going out into the fields of learning,
We shake the dew from the grasses.
All is new.
The paths we make through the wet grasses shine
As if with light.

They go where we take them, where they go.
Slow wings unfold, scarcely any
Motion happens but our heavy seeking.

Ant labors, hopper leaps away; too early for the bee,
The spider's silk hypotheses unfold
Tenacious, tenable.

Conception

Death did not come to my mother
Like an old friend.
She was a mother, and she must
Conceive him.

Up and down the bed she fought crying
Help me, but death
Was a slow child
Heavy. He

Waited. When he was born
We took and tired him, now he is ready
To do his good in the world.

He has my mother's features.
He can go among strangers
To save lives.

Toward I

When you turned away your attention
I turned mine away,
And I said, out of whatever corner of your interest
You have put me for safe keeping,
I will escape into peril.
And then the full bearing of your attention
In floodlight will veer upon me.
Oh, there you are.
And about time.

By some syllogism I still bring
Vengeance to myself that I see myself
Harried and at large down corridors
Of incapacity and perturbation where
Your presence, could it turn to me, would say,
Oh, there you are.
But the attention
Of your presence is diffused.

Toward II

Go out a little from yourself as you sit here,
Maybe to the path outside the window
Maybe to an idea,
Or to in the next row an absorbing form.
Reject most of the lecture,
Most of your thought, most that the window bears,
Maybe the whole morning. There is being sifted
The sand of your time, turning as you turn.

I am beside you and we are exchanging
Several aspects of the ideas of history,
From their glosses there are being sifted
Sands of a time only becoming yours.
Sift me away and sift the whole morning.
Some day, not accountable, you may look down
To see in your palm as on a field of history
The grain of time you recognize as yours.

Family

When you swim in the surf off Seal Rocks, and your family
Sits in the sand
Eating potato salad, and the undertow
Comes which takes you out away down
To loss of breath loss of play and the power of play
Holler, say
Help, help, help. Hello, they will say,
Come back here for some potato salad.

It is then that a seventeen year old cub
Cruising in a helicopter from Antigua,
A jackstraw expert speaking only Swedish
And remote from this area as a camel, says
Look down there, there is somebody drowning.
And it is you. You say, yes, yes,
And he throws you a line.
This is what is called the brotherhood of man.

Away

Never going off, always here, I
Never say goodbye. You may
Leave over and over, for good,
For the weekend, for my life; I
Wave and cry

What is my life but your leaving?
Giving a brief biography of my life, I say
Each year they are off, all of them,
Goodbye, goodbye,
Yet here I stay

As in 1940, 41, 58, 59, 60, 70,
Now again they are going away.
Born yet unlearned in travel,
Each sacramental day
I give over
And they take it away.

and Selected

Herald

Delivers papers to the doors of sleep
Tosses up news upon the shores of sleep
In the day's damp, in the street's swamp wades deep
And is himself the boy drowned, drowned with sleep.

Crosses to the corner with the lamp
Already dark, even asleep the lamp,
Treads in the wet grass, wares, leaps as in swamp
The gutters dark with darkening of the lamp

Hears only the thud and thud against the doors
Of the news falling asleep against the doors,
The slip and drip of mist on the two shores,
Sees without light or sight the coasts of doors.

Sees at a door a light, Herald, Sir?
Wakes to the whistle and light, Herald, Sir?
To the latch lifted and the face's blur
Wakes; wakes coin, day, greeting, Herald, Sir.

Solo

The structure of music as an art behind that morning glory
Behind that oak door is perpetually refounded,
Sets to in the fresher hours toward recognition,
Is this I? and is astounded.

The bar laborious rises above the breadman's whistle,
It is I, it is music written and revealed.
In the half step and broken note, am I wrong? no, it is I
Loud though concealed.

In this eventual song, this étude, this caprice espagnole
Is not a mountain, not a wind or breath, nor a morning glory or door,
Yet hear in the way it is piling up it is sometimes I
That the keys are climbing for.

I swear it will win through the kimono sleeves and the street's ply,
By whatever chances music is surprised,
And will set up in the vines, along the wind, sound that is I,
Founded and recognized.

Seer

The psychic metaphysician sat tight in the white
Shine of the rocks outside Riverside,
It was like living in a world of mirrors
The left hand rocks and leaves so took the light,
The left of cornflakes in the kitchenette
So took the light.

Is it wind or is it a new year, asked the psychic metaphysician
Resting his hand upon the parlor chair, and the flare
Of answers long lying in that dust dazzled him,
The left hand cups and mirrors so took the light,
It was like living in a world of answers
The hand so took the light.

I shall be prodigal with thine information,
The psychic metaphysician knelt and spelt,
Changing fifty cents to forty on his sign,
It swung against the porch and took the light,
It was like living in a world of sight
The sign so took the light.

After This, Sea

This is as far as the land goes, after this it is sea.
This is where my father stopped, being no sailor,
Being no Beowulf, nor orient spice hungry
Here he let horizons come quietly to rest.

What he fled is past and over,
Raftered roof and quilted cover,
The known street and the known face,
The stale place.

This is as far as the land goes, here we are at length
Facing back on the known street and face, all flight
Spent before our time in building the new towns,
Letting these last horizons come quietly to rest.

We have a special pressing need
We of the outer border breed
To climb these hills we cannot flee
To swim in this sea.

This is as far as the land goes, here the coast ranges
Hard and brown stand down to hold the ocean,
Here the winds are named for saints and blow on leaves
Small, young, yellow, few, but bound to be ancestral.

Nowhere are so still as here
Four horizons, or so clear.
Whatever we make here, whatever find,
We cannot leave behind.

Men Friday

This water is for ships, that they cleave it,
That the grooves leap
Cleanly at the bow and clearly leave it,
As freight is borne upon the face of the deep.

This ground is for feet, that they tread it,
That commerce start
In the dust, and the feet spread it
Counter to counter, paradise to port.

Came ever out of the blue a free faring
Wind upon this strand,
It would start and wonder at the sea bearing
Keel prints, at the heel prints in the sand.

Upon Twelve

Now has been contrived in the increasing noonday
Some show of order wherein to be at rest,
Some stilling of the need that space be tended
That time be pressed.

Where in our path was the ambitious clutter of morning,
The leaf shadow and stir, the brush and broom,
Now at the base of trees is a clean sunlight,
At the door, room.

We shall sit with minds quiet, with the loftiness, though cooler,
That the sun has for its meridian,
In the fine short space before the roof eastward
Darkens again.

Driver Saying

Lady hold your horses, sit down in your seat,
Wrap your feet around the leg of the chair,
Even in my heart I can feel your heart beat.

We move, however, on schedule of need
Of the general public, see, standing on the corner there,
Holding hats, lifting canes, cutting down our speed.

Lady calm down, we'll be stopping and starting
On your nerves and my brakes ten corners more,
There'll be plenty feet to watch climbing up and departing.

There is also a good signboard at the Filmart
To look at and keep your mind on when we pass there.
Lady, even in second I can hear your heart.

Enlightenment

I wish we could take a statistic with more grace, beloved,
I wish it would circle out in our minds to the very brim,
And we could be illumined by data one by one, as by candles,
As by the cheerful faces of cherubim.

But see we respond only to archangelic doctrine,
Look up and glow at the actual pronouncement of grace,
Swallow at once all the high powered radiance,
And let the commandments shine upon the face.

This is a tremendous lot of revelation we gather,
Beloved, and beam at it in the proper spirit.
Nevertheless I wish we had one or two facts to go by,
And a less arclighted kingdom to inherit.

For Futures

When the lights come on at five o'clock on street corners
That is Evolution by the bureau of power,
That is a fine mechanic dealing in futures:
For the sky is wide and warm upon that hour,

But like the eyes that burned once at sea bottom,
Widening in the gloom, prepared for light,
The ornamental standards, the glazed globes softly
Perceive far off how probable is night.

Row

Some of the roofs are of Hopi Indian decision,
They cut square into the sky with plaster,
The tan edge going up two stories past the windows
And turning north and east for straight cement horizon.

Some have old noble English temper peaked,
Alternate red and green shingles but getting the drift,
Gabled to peer out of a possible anciently fallen snow,
And clear superior against gray sky.

All of them look west and take in sunset,
Keep their ferns warm the length of supper,
Sparkle their cups of milk and all accompany
With aerial music that evening sun go down.

Premiere

The searchlights ask the stars nothing
Among them going,
Tell them nothing, their sign of show
Being for more particular sight below.

Show, show, say they to the sight
Through the lamplight
Raying cloud, cloud, and cloud to wake and start
The after dinner heart.

There is stir in the driveways and rustle of departing,
With the hearts starting,
And sight can almost see, ear hear, at the lights' core
Gathering, shining, what the lights are searching for.

Made Shine

This face had no use for light, took none of it,
Grew cavernous against stars, bore into noon
A dark of midnight by its own resources.

Yet where it lay in sleep, where the pillow held it
With the blind plaster over it and the four walls
Keeping the night carefully, it was undone.

Sixty-watt light, squared to a window frame,
Across a well of air, across wind and window
Leaped and made shine the dark face in its sleep.

Market Report on Cotton Gray Goods

Cotton gray goods quiet and firmer
Sold in small amounts at steady prices.
Some were unaware at distance from the market
How those bolts reflected prepossessed their cost per head
And quieted.

Raw silk was unchanged and rayon yarns actively
Lapped up demand that firmed to cream just,
Rose with time just topping at the market,
A calm waylaying and surrendering, a portion sped
And quieted.

Wool goods mills started showing suitings,
Bustled up a test drama of art and taste,
The higher life at slightly higher prices
Suggested by an exact at-homeness of stripe, bred
And quieted.

After luncheon the stocks prevailed further
In a muted influence and exercise of will
Tanging the office airs like manifests
Of season, which they were, unfolding spread
And quieted.

Conveyed not only crop but moon quarter,
State of mortgage, not only ground but floor
Of wage, put over to mind the color of climate,
Fence-rail and stool both, corn and boughten bread,
Yet quieted.

Conveyed, so listening was that atmosphere, a dry
Air that comes seldom at seaboard but then has absorbed
A catalogue of some possible warm accents and beliefs,
Conveyed warp brought to grief and packing rioted
Yet quieted.

Quieted in the streets of afternoon the dry interior air,
Occasioning a steadying of burlap in the late day,
Through the good offices of the rolls themselves
Their own substantial nature weaved and undersaid
And quieted.

Committee Report on Smoke Abatement in Residential Area

Prevailing winds in this area blow
The fume of life away.
The mesh bag carriers when they go to shop
Can look around the day.

A ceiling blue maintains a working breath
Of ozone in the street,
And blinds blow inward with a birdy note
Of sun complete.

However, three or four months out of the year
Prevailing winds abate,
And the smoke of interest enters
Closet however strait.

Today is such a one. Some off in the smoke
Keep the miles dim.
And some at home bake black enough for the
    kids when they get there
Bread of the brothers Grimm.

Government Injunction Restraining Harlem Cosmetic Co.

They say La Jac Brite Pink Skin Bleach avails not,
They say its Orange Beauty Glow does not glow,
Nor the face grow five shades lighter nor the heart
Five shades lighter. They say no.

They deny good luck, love, power, romance, and inspiration
From La Jac Brite ointment and incense of all kinds,
And condemn in writing skin brightening and whitening
And whitening of minds.

There is upon the federal trade commission a burden of glory
So to defend the fact, so to impel
The plucking of hope from the hand, honor from the complexion,
Sprite from the spell.

Moonrise in City Park

Here you have sky high one wall
And one at its shoulder to the sixth floor,
Here you have the two story house with the colonial door;
And says the sign, Beauty Culture,
Beauty Culture, says the sign.

Here you have the stack of dentist offices,
Here shoulder high the Philharmonic wall:
The nice culture of the mouth and music. Over all
The sign glows beauty,
Beauty, glows the sign.

Here rises from the blank and black the moon,
The blond beauty at the colonial door,
The bright blond face ascending from the sixth floor,
With the sign suggesting culture,
Culture, suggesting the sign.

From this park bench look up and say divine,
To the dark levels speak and say divine,
To the moon whisper also and say divine,
And the sign will join you, saying Beauty
Culture, saying the sign.

Beach Party
Given by T. Shaughnessy for the Sisters

Seven nuns went wading in the sea,
They wore no shoes,
They lined up along the shore and the shore washed out
And flooded back to the very knee.
A rough but good shore and sea.

The seaweed and the wimple habits were,
Close and alive,
Both cumbrous but of will designed and worn.
For every nun the sea was good to her,
And alike their habits were.

It was so rough a day, like cormorants more
You would have thought
The nuns would take to nest, but still they cried and stayed.
They were like to the devout sea, and to the shore
They sisters were.

Peak Activity in Boardwalk Ham Concession

What was that they heard past the peal
Of the booth's bells and the squeal
Round the turned edges of the wide red sucker?
Past the surf of the game wheel
The surf of ocean.

Here's your hot ham folks, tells
To the peal of the booth's bells,
To the round red face round the red sucker,
The driven voice that spells
Ham to the ocean.

What was that the licker heard
That her tongue slow on the third
Round tasted there more of salt than strawberry sucker,
Marking without a word
The lick of ocean?

Here's the turn of the wheel folks, cries
To the wheel's fall and rise,
To the fall of dimes and the face of the all day sucker,
The driven voice to the rise
And fall of ocean.

Polo Match. Sunday, 2 P.M.

Polo has that gravy look game,
Tough brushed out and thus adaptable,
Rare, but thick and springy,
Thought up as a grist well-chewed by a gold tooth.

The soppers of that gravy save all Sunday for it
And picnic at its bounds; they sit on Sunday papers
And pay no fee but the warning distant gasp
Of the multitude so good for a good pony.

Polo picks up an area of turf and takes it
Right down the lines, it biases the natural green,
It goals the very day, with evidence
Of practice flavoring that efficiency.

Riders have the watchers licking chops,
Not only in the pleased way of relatives and friends,
But in the ready gust of the professional eaters
Taking the taste up deftly from a distance.

Gravy, gravy of the haunch and flexion
Sliding and righting, at a chewable degree
Soaks down the Sunday aft in a feast for the breadwinners,
The breadwinners winning it all up deep to saturation.

Committee Decision on Pecans for Asylum

Orphans are to have instead of walnuts
From a state two thousand and twenty miles distant,
Pecans from home.

The Santa Claus committee up and authorized
One ton of black walnuts for the orphan stockings
But found ton bottom bad.

Took the word of the agricultural inspectors
Somebody had been led on a bad buy
Pulling the whiskers of the jolly saint.

Tossed out the lying samples suitable and savory,
Eligible for orphans, and acknowledged
Better pecans from home.

> Orchards of home, the orphan house and home own,
> Sweeten in the cold for their first hard teeth,
> The fluted sweet brittle and home grown
> Substance in sheath.
>
> Kernels of home, frosting with Christmas cheer,
> Crispen not for an individual mantel and tongue
> But a massed patriot lunge and lick this year,
> The hungry younger democrat so does long.
>
> Shake out intending crackle over that brisk brick,
> Making to matron and minor mildly known
> How under the burnish and the bluff of stick
> The sweet is grown.

The committee saint withdraws the possibility
Of a foreign exotic flavor for the ribs,
Of black nut crack,

And goes back of necessity to its original and time tried
Local lesson of the nature of good
Pecans from home.

Art Gallery Closing Time

Steps never went away so far as when they carried
Mr. and Mrs. Smith out of the gallery of the museum of art.
Steps went down out of morning and one could not turn round and
 ascend them.

They went down into evening out of the gallery of the palace of art
And so brought one into Mr. MacGregor's chaos,
A fine thriving city with car tracks and stop signs every which way.

They went out into the red network of evening,
One white marble portion after another nimbly rounding
Away from the morning marshes and flamingoes in the palace of the
 legion of art.

Now That April's There

Coming up to the boulevard stop on the slant,
The poplars standing off along,
The white proceeding and as white crossed,
One would have to look a west sun in the eye.

Picking up after La Cienega the long quiet,
The porch lights flying, still as they are,
The cars staying along the curb north and south quiet,
One would have to go straight chin deep in light on the level tracts.

Stopping for ice, bouncing in short against the red paint,
The store building facing up like a bastille,
One would have to get breath to look off down the street,
Down the low roofs, races of pavement, meadows of evening.

And so I would if there I were, there I would take
One into another the long flat avenues of the angels,
Lower than the west light, the luminous levels,
There through the shiny shallows remember that one dimension.

The Lighting of the Street Lights

Corinthian is the light they see by,
It renews Corinth in the fall of blue,
Polishing the car tops and the carob trees
In marble custom and the linear shade.

When they run out to get ice cream it is the light that shines
over them,
Fluted in length; it illumines
The face of the mantel clock when no one asks the time,
Abides that round of dark over them.

It is white on pedestal in classic vein
In the first pitching of morning when they come home elate,
Column burning with a cool ancient flare,
The light they see by, the Corinthian.

The Lighting of a Small Fire in the Grate

When oak is burning, that is warming
At earth's fire, grown up in wood and established.
What when
Newspaper stews and fizzles in the grate?

That, let a Barrymore conclude, is a wet humanity,
A print of a thousand feet and eyes, all damp
But lit
To keep a spirit flaring at its heat.

That is history not yet a wood, but a good
Pulp nipping at the flame, a personal endeavour
Of persons in the news
To serve and blaze.

Moonrise in a Lumber Yard

New wood under the sun will blister for heat
And split for dryness, warped in the woodyard,
Under the satellite it does not blister or split
But lies as cut, neat hard and fit.

The satellite implies to the new wood this
That it will have to take no nails nor saw in its side,
No nor filler nor prime nor what coat you please,
But lie as it is, wide and at ease.

The satellite assures with its frank white address
That this is what the wood is hewn for and displayed,
To repose in the glimmer and shine in the yards stacked,
In the balmy press inlaid, intact.

Nine O'Clock Show

Going into the show one heard nothing but closing sounds,
Doors closing, shutters drawing down,
Except before the palace and ice cream parlor
One heard the closing of the town,
One heard the shades and shops and nightfall drawing down.

But after Harlow listen what has arisen,
The rustle of feet in leaves and leaves in black,
The suck of straws and slam of a screen door rising,
Rising the racket of frogs in the waking black,
In the town in the field in the heart and the whole way back.

Preliminary to Classroom Lecture

My quiet kin, must I affront you
With a telling tongue?
Will not a mission or request content you
To move as you belong
The fields of doubt among?

The voice to burden down a tale upon you
Were indolent with din.
Would better ask and have the answer from you.
And would you then begin
Querying too, querying, my quiet kin?

Purchase of Lodging for the Night

Evil hemmed the curtains and swung in with them slightly
When slightly the western air blew in.
Evil starched the pillow, it was evil
So firmly feathered.

Tourist from high road came in and put his bag down,
Washed his face, read his magazine,
And there came evil numbering the page twenty,
Singing in the light bulb.

All night turned when he turned, looked across the mirror,
Crowed at cock-crow,
But lay still in the linoleum and hem of curtain
When he went down to breakfast.

Purchase of a Hat to Wear in the Sun

Sombrero is comfort because it keeps thought under foot,
Keeps the personal shadow to heel,
Keeps the stride covered,
Covers brain cosily from reel.

Paces along in a degree of sun put to it
To force hard, and under, the addle pate,
And yet filters all that compulsion
Compelled to its own colonial gait.

Provides the porch of shade and colonnade for thought
To rock in, surveying the domain not too continuously,
And steadies spot of domain out of sun,
Even where's none other to survey.

Tips the sombrero on, the mortal booted,
And travels under it, thinking
Just enough coolly and in shadow
To survive under blessing without blinking.

Purchase of a Blue, Green, or Orange Ode

Jake's store past Pindaric mountain
Over the wash is the only place in a day's ride
To get odes at except close to Mesa City side.

He has one glass a dusty one there
Full of blue green and orange odes sticky but o k,
And many come by on that account that way.

Scramble down off the hot flats, swallow a lot of universal wind,
Hear that lone freight pushing around sandy acre,
And they need for the slow swipes one green jawbreaker.

A slug of sweet, a globe of a barber's pole,
A suck of a human victory out of a crowd,
Sugared, colored, out of a jar, an ode.

So Graven

Simplicity so graven hurts the sense.
The monumental and the simple break
And the great tablets shatter down in deed.

Every year the quick particular jig
Of unresolved event moves in the mind,
And there's the trick simplicity has to win.

Contained

The beautiful intense light of intense morning
Allows the fullest speculation toward the day,
The reach of every hand and hope outward
To come what may.

The noon the afternoon the night and after
Are all implied in the free life of green,
And morning's self-contained. But looks to windward
For more to be seen.

Neither events complete nor sun's attainment
Are enough thought for the green to gather in.
It's the pure black hope of morning so greens it,
The notion of again.

Bloom

The steamfitter comes home in a pink cloud plainly
Keeps his helmet clapped on his head vainly,
It's a new day, season, and 7 A.M. only.

The quinces ripen in their most lurid blossoms,
They thicken on every side the streetcar pathways,
The dogtired steamfitter gets home between them.

One plush of quince at his own door he will doff to,
Take in the dawn his hard steel helmet off to,
But bush will not bend or petal blow, it's so early.

Gypsy

The entire country is overrun with private property, the gypsy king
 said.
I don't know if this is true,
I believe in the gypsy kingship though.

The lost tribes of my own nation
Rove and rove.
In red and yellow rough and silent move.

I believe
The majesty pot mending, copper smith
On the hundred highways, nothing to do with.

And black eyes, black I never saw,
Searching out the pocket lines of cloth
The face lines and the furrows of belief.

It's a curious fact, Stephan, King, if you are made to doubt
Aegyptian vision on the Jersey shore.
Property's private as ever, ever.

Opal

The steamfitter had no notion of buying an opal,
But a stone comes sudden in its meaning often.

He looked for a new watch, that part of his life, there was none,
He had to furnish his own time sense.

But this opal. Fire of time that burned in the antique reaches,
Roman omen, power of the sooth.

How comes so much actual straight evil into an opal?
Fix on a streak of bad luck, it goes out.

How comes so much red, then green, into an opal?
There aren't those colors in a glass of milk.

His wife didn't want the jewel but he bought it
And took that burden on, which fate forebore.

Friend

As I was going past Capstan's Well
I met a man in a woolen reefer,
A friend of my friend's.
What was his disposition?

He was bald as a bat
Blind as an egg
Bent as a lion, bold as a bird.
A singular complex of idiosyncratic qualities.

Then let me explain, said the man in the reefer,
I too am a friend of a friend and a dream of a dreamer,
A classical character often.
And often beloved.

Well Made

Familiar to our readers
In all its special vein
Is the form of the tale in the author's careful form.
The incident beginning
And then begun again
With love and care to keep the cockles warm.

The palpitant unfoldment
And dear and sudden end,
The shape of the tale in the author's burning hope
Familiar to our readers,
But not the blind
Looking around of the mind for the shape.

Forecast

All our stones like as much sun as possible.
Along their joints run both solar access and decline
In equal splendor, like a mica chipping
At every beat, being sun responsible.

How much sun then do you think is due them?
Or should say, how much sun do you think they are apt to have?
It has misted at their roots for some days now,
The gray glamour addressing itself to them.

I should think possible that it go on misting likewise
A good way into next year, or time as they have it,
A regular cool season every day for our stones.
Not a streak that low of any sun or longed surprise.

Merchant Marine

Where is the world? not about.
The world is in the heart
And the heart is clogged in the sea lanes out of port.

Not in the work or the west,
Not in the will or the wriest
Task is the world. It is all seaward.

Chart is the world, a sheet
In the hand and a paper page,
A rendable tissue of sea lanes, there is the heart.

Players

Into the spacious bay the sun of afternoon
Shone,
And there two people, a man with a beard and a woman without,
    were playing
At cards alone.

Lake traffic, line traffic, pine, plain traffic all around them
Presided,
Roared but soft, rushed but not
Into the window many-sided,

Looking for a game to play, a war to win, some sort of magnificent
    errand
To be done;
While the spadebeard took easily a trick
Already a century won.

Dolor

When swimming and croquet are in full sway, dolor
Asserts itself, rocks on the porches its own whited color.

Dolor dismayed with one life after another
Tells its tally, but never tells enough.

Never gets the last iota pat, never gets
Veronica buried, thought of her too late.

Extend, dolor, extend, assert, and let
No one walk to the postoffice in the middle of this.

Maintain on one sunporch, in one mild
Summer, one dismay unreconciled.

The Thoroughgoing

He killed and kept.
He doused the capitol city in kerosene,
He chopped the maples up for firewood
And then it was the city they kept warm.
All winter warmed preserved and kept
For him.

He told the city fathers: die, and they
Died with unwillingness and shock and met again
Next weekday morning for the usual course
Of minor and perhaps a major bill.
All morning voted and vetoed the village ways and means
For him.

He had his uncle understand the old was dead,
Laid down the old man's bay in earth for a leaner muscle,
And grayly from the grave came home to find
The glitter of watch chain crossed his uncle's dinner.
Saved for him. The heirloom worn aloft and soft and now and still
Saved for him.

The Sympathizers

To this man, to his boned shoulders
Came the descent of pain.
All kinds
Cruel, blind, dear, horrid, hallowed,
Rained, again, again.

To this small white blind boned face
Wherever it was
Descended
The blows of pain, it took as it were blinded,
As it were made for this.

We were there. We uneasy
Did not know if it were.
Knew neither
The reason nor the man nor whether
To share, or to beware.

Loser

A gracious number of darkwitted thieves
Stole all I had, in a pack as thick as that.
I was so disappointed I rocked as I sat.

I chewed on a straw hoping it would get sweeter.
It got drier and drier
And gradually caught on fire.

I spat it out, nothing left to chew,
I looked up the street and I looked down,
I saw that everything was really gone.

The people who got the goods enjoyed them I guess
For they never brought them back fourfold in a dray
As I expected them to until this day.

Lucifer Alone

One rat across the floor and quick to floor's a breeze,
But two a whisper of a human tongue.
One is a breath, two voice;
And one a dream, but more are dreamed too long.

Two are the portent which we may believe at length,
And two the tribe we recognize as true.
Two are the total, *they* saying and *they* saying,
So we must ponder what we are to do.

For every scuttle of motion in the corner of the eye
Some thought of thought is asked in us indeed,
But of two, more: there we have likeness moving,
And there knowledge therefore, and therefore creed.

What Followed

In all happiness and peace of mind
The man spoke a villainy, he was sore at it
And would have it back but it was gone already,
Ducked in the pool of the past and there no diver,
It was done for and he with it, he said.

But the very villainy got up of itself,
It was so light it ran, and he after it,
Asking everybody as he ran where it went to,
All had seen it and spoke of it to him,
They knew him by it.

When one summer eve in another county
He met up with the villainy at a band concert,
Asked how it did, said here am I
My whole life and place of life changed by chasing you,
He found he held its leash, it was his seeing eye
Purchased and instructed.

All Hallow

The lady in the unbecoming bonnet
Let down her weeping hair.
She saw the broomstick and the witch upon it
Riding there.

The wind was full of bottles and the air
Aggressive as a shell.
The lady watched about her everywhere
The sallyings of hell.

The little boys stopped ringing at the bell
As she came homeward sadly. They had her cat
Spitting and mewing, a black one: lady,
Whose cat is that?

Corner

Who knows his way around a corner clear as day
When the lights let down,
Millinery store becomes a den,
Merchandise sobers coldly over town?
Who then?

The running boys then with the spurt of noise,
Not to look and not to buy
But to lead the way
Of every empty corner under sky
Into the opposites of day.

Confidence

Thank you for your kind attention.
    How the ear can rest upon the heart.
    The long bolster of a life story
    Fresh at the ear and in every mention
    Full of comfort.

Rest and attend again, for if more beating
    Trembles in the heart to attend
    It will be an undertale and differing story,
    The second speech, a plea, and the more fleeting,
    Told to the friend.

Midweek

Plentiful people went to the Cadillac drawing,
My ticket was number nine seven two seven one,
And my friend's ticket was number nine seven two seven two,
Certainly a lucky number and easy to remember.
I thought of it all through the film, and I like Greer Garson.

O heaven when the lights went up, the table trundled in,
The number called didn't even begin with a nine.
There wasn't even that much respite of hope after the happy ending.
That is the kind of change the brave buckle
Time and again to.

All those people heart-rent and rustling,
I wished the upper lights would not look down so,
The curtain not so aquamarine, the manager not in tuxedo,
Me not so pale. I wished the second feature
Dark and dreadful.

Outside

Ever saw sidewalk uninterpreted?
This is one.
The Rialto sidewalk with environs
Makes no sense.

What does it give sea legs after a sea picture?
Gumpapers.
What does it give spurs after range riding?
A slippery basement tilt.

Any other sidewalk fits the foot,
Takes in and out of doors and miles away
Any number of acknowledging steps,
You lead, I follow,

I take you up on that.
But this cementy floor makes no legitimate offer.
It extends for the night flight survivors
To alight, not awake, but walk over.

Dancer

The foot and knee of the dancer
Must learn the room he is in.
Must seek in the room of the dancer
Its special pleasure.

Whether of draw and rise
Whether of cramp and fawn
Whether of extensive and ambling leisure,
The identifiable measure.

The room of the dancer changes,
The way-stations of his ways
Collapse from hall ranges
To tiled bays

And back expand, flicker.
The toe's to tell
To the doubting heart of the dancer
If these mean well.

To tell to the cord of the dancer
What footing and follow is
On every fleeting platform,
And what platform his.

The Disturbed

They drummed salvation in the darker districts
And a man cried Save me.
They closed the circle up, he was not a sober sinner.

He pushed at the corner crowd and came at them.
Save me.
They closed the placards round that said Repent.

Easy easy there, the tall young preacher murmured.
Save me.
See my scars, I repent, replied the desperate sinner.

Pull up my shirt and see the scars on my stomach.
Save me.
They are my sins, count them, the sinner cried.

Then to the increased crowd the three soft
Sopranos started singing Judgment,
Jubilee for the unsaved and the unsober.

Illumination

The light burns in the foliage, but the bushes
Will not burn.
The light flares and fades but the bushes in the dark
Assume no single spark.

The willows in the water drink and survive
Greening the channel water.
The black world moist and green
Where the light burns to be seen.

The incendiary mind of light pours its array
Leaf over leaf the light.
The full foliage thickened, the green bough bloomed
Will not be consumed.

Forward

Impervious to its pledge the human heart
Looks not to forward or to rear but sinks
Into an instant and there drifts entire.
How forward are the suns that rise again.

The pledge now called, the sources now are spent,
The scene impoverished and the heart secure,
What's time that lets not well enough alone?
How forward are the suns that rise again.

Perfection can insist percent's complete,
The round and perfect heart retire from love.
How forward are the suns that rise again.

None

A nothing out of which to create a new
Was never nothing enough for a new, never
Empty lost lone nought enough
To come clean new in any morning light.

Always in that limbo wide as it was,
Deep, down, as it was, somebody lay
Qualifying any possible creation.
Toppled in that void tossed there, and woke.

Son

Men have their alien sons and love them,
The dear fist clenched in theirs,
The foreign taste fed at their table,
The wayward walking in their name.
They love their handsome son.

But they hate the foreign, though an open
Five-fingered hand like theirs,
The gall taste deep as another nation,
The ugly accent in an alien name.
Hate all but him, dear father, and dear son.

Holiday

Returning from the north, I saw the sun returning
In the same car.
Back to our indigent county we retreated
From the summer war.

All us vacationers, dead, alive, burnt,
Said as we rode
That to live up to the Fourth of July, Christmas
Would have to be pretty good.

And we rode in the memory
Of the rockets' red glare
Blazing and disintegrating to our vision
In the soft summer air.

But the sun was recollecting in its wide glance,
Passive and regional,
Necessities of a colder danger, with the chance
Of a warmer festival.

The Day the Winds

The day the winds went underground I gasped for breath,
Did not you?—oxygen gone from the chest wall,
Nostrils pinched in the scant weather, strictest
Sort of equilibrium at street corners.

It was a pity. Who could walk in the hills now
Or run for a train? The water in a storm
Ran down the sides of buildings and the bark of trees
Straight down, like tears.

In the first days it was not so desperate;
I remember, though short of breath,
Thinking with relief in the dense quiet,
Fall will be quiet.

But more and more as the streets clogged with traffic
And the smog of the city's production lay on its eyes,
One could notice persons burrowing, hearts hammering,
Toward the risks of the wind.

Sale

Went into a shoestore to buy a pair of shoes,
There was a shoe salesman humming the blues
Under his breath; over his breath
Floated a peppermint lifesaver, a little wreath.

I said please I need a triple-A,
And without stopping humming or swallowing his lifesaver away
He gave one glance from toe to toe
And plucked from the mezzanine the very shoe.

Skill of the blessed, that at their command
Blue and breathless comes to hand
To send, from whatever preoccupation, feet
Implacably shod into the perfect street.

Summer

When I came to show you my summer cottage
By the resounding sea,
We found a housing project building around it,
Two stories being painted green row after row
So we were set in an alley.

But there is the sea I said, off the far corner
Through that vacant land;
And there the pile of prefabricating panels
And the cement blocks swiftly
Rose in the sand.

So darkened the sunlit alley.
Ovid, Arthur, oh Orion I said, run
Take Rags with you, send me back
News of the sea.
So they did, vanishing away off and shouting.

Belief

Mother said to call her if the H bomb exploded
And I said I would, and it about did
When Louis my brother robbed a service station
And lay cursing on the oily cement in handcuffs.

But by that time it was too late to tell Mother,
She was too sick to worry the life out of her
Over *why why*. Causation is sequence
And everything is one thing after another.

Besides, my other brother, Eddie, had got to be President,
And you can't ask too much of one family.
The chances were as good for a good future
As bad for a bad one.

Therefore it was surprising that, as we kept the newspapers from Mother,
She died feeling responsible for a disaster unverified,
Murmuring, in her sleep as it seemed, the ancient slogan
Noblesse oblige.

Ride

It's not my world, I grant, but I made it.
It's not my ranch, lean oak, buzzard crow,
Not my fryers, mixmaster, well-garden.
And now it's down the road and I made it.

It's not your rackety car but you drive it.
It's not your four-door, top-speed, white-wall tires,
Not our state, not even, I guess, our nation,
But now it's down the road, and we're in it.

Reason

Said, Pull her up a bit will you, Mac, I want to unload there.
Said, Pull her up my rear end, first come first serve.
Said, Give her the gun, Bud, he needs a taste of his own bumper.
Then the usher came out and got into the act:

Said, Pull her up, pull her up a bit, we need this space, sir.
Said, For God's sake, is this still a free country or what?
You go back and take care of Gary Cooper's horse
And leave me handle my own car.

Saw them unloading the lame old lady,
Ducked out under the wheel and gave her an elbow,
Said, All you needed to do was just explain;
Reason, Reason is my middle name.

Education

I would sit in the window's ledge
At Los Angeles High School
To watch the pecking sparrows
To hear the bickering girls
Their warm and lively life.

The sun that shone thereon
Would draw to warmest life
The coldest bone and silent
To ruffle in its dust
Bicker its edge of sun.

Now what shall I say of the cat
That sprang the pecking sparrows
What of the aunt that ate
The slightest bickering girls
What of the heart

Once warmed by delicate rays
Now sheltering all that sun
Till it would bless and blaze
A thousand windows in
A universe of schools?

Student

Who is that student pale and importunate
Whom I have left with a heavy burden and forgotten all about?
Who wakes me as I fall asleep, asking
What I want done with the job now that the year's over.

And indeed I remember now he has been doing all my work,
Setting up the experiments, kidding the bystanders,
Puzzling the problems, and I have forgotten him
Till now too late, and must wait until morning.

Who is he? my thought which I deny until the dark,
Or one literal person I have now forgot
Who, early in the alphabet, recited
More than I could learn until tonight?

Ten Dreamers in a Motel

1

Some people said the cabin
Wouldn't hold us two,
Two hundred and forty pounds,
Two hundred and twenty-two.

But note wherever we moved
Back or face to face
Outside the windows flew
Hundreds of butterflies.

So that within our walls,
Walls that denied us well,
Glimmered the wing that tells
All things are possible

To elephant and elephant
Stalking exact apart,
The centennial memory
Of a light heart.

2

At this dinner I was telling you about
Next door to this motel
Was your pal your host,
And me, and a mother, daughter
Come to greet you back, how they loved you.

She for the past as if a bowl of carnations
Sat with the chicken;
She for the chicken;
He for the silverware.

The lines of life which moved between you
Like toy tramcars
Were also like toy speedsters
Building up speed.
An electric party.

Except, between us, you
And me met to greet you back,
Was absence still.
A freedom free enough to kill.

3

One day we started out
To pick up driftwood. I was interested
In a housing project there, I had heard a lecture
Illuminating the beach like lightning.
It was my concern
To raise on the shingle rows of boards
On which the great foundations could be built.

Rather, I found the shanties were up already,
And indeed down already, every one
Empty to the tide as if just then
They had been lived in but would live no more.
I turned round.
If I had been looking south I looked north
East west I turned.

4

On which of the many hills
Of suburbs out beyond the State Fair on Saturday morning
Did we pasture our goats?
Up down over the Marguerite Street district
We saw the angel ladders behind before us
But not that field in which our thoughts were bound.

Conceive if you can the animal desolation
Which besieged us on all sides other districts than our own.
We were, myself and self, not enough to ensure
Any comfort of company, but one who will say
So it is, and not let me deny, say
Let us go back by the municipal railway.

5

Carombed out of town in a comedy chase fashion
Police oblique to our path, and statues
Wheeled over, through Harlem, and all more wasteful as we went,
And ended up at this tourist cabin,
Its outlook, so it was said, restful.

Went to the window,
Pushed aside the curtains and there saw
That countryside we longed for: rocks
Steep slopes of rocks, rubble and rusk of rocks.
What is it? and you said, *moraine*.

6

When we came back all the underpasses were flooded,
Highway 40 blocked off
And six inches of water at the supermarket.
So it was necessary to go round by the byroads.

So it was that we came to our street from a different view,
Saw our neighborhood from aside and below,
Stacked up the hill our houses in their shrub,
Their windows empty as an evening sky.

And so it was we saw that they dwelt without us,
Endured merrily as bastions against our presence,
Persons of note and self in the rainy evening,
Lampless and starless.

7

I saw a field of folk in fit array,
A circus field, or fair,
A tumbler tintwister and autocourt carnival
Brought for the day.

Among which I went, larking and singing,
Crowding and wandering, till
Where was I? everybody wandered
While I stood still, longing

To find myself out, there to find,
And in relief
I felt at my shoulder, straight beside me,
Father or friend.

But it was not, but a strange
Present person who stood,
To whom that field fair and carnival
And I, he said, belonged.

8

I went to consult a psychiatrist on this morning,
A nervous woman, whose curly-headed four-year-old child
Played in the room, sitting staunchly
On a great medical scales.

I defended myself thus. It looks as if
All this weariness came from too much work,
But rather I think it a problem of person,
Friend or foe, fortune of parent or pardon.

The nervous psychiatrist ran her hand through her hair
And glanced at her watch. Have you taken a trip lately,
It would do you good, and take your mother with you,
She needs it more than you do.

Then I laughed to hear my own prescription
Given to myself with such good humor
In the grey weariness. But then she said also,
Take with you also my curly-headed four-year-old child.

9

I said to my iron class, I am desperate, desperate,
You must learn and you will not.
Each by each I looked to into the light and said
You are fast in darkness.

Each to each I said I am desperate, desperate.
Then one rose from his seat and sat beside me
Touching my hand and saying, out of his daylight,
Do not despair.

10

Midway stayed at a court between there and here
Where woodsmoke rose up straight into the sky
Cabin by cabin the suppers cooking
Far as the eye could see, the courts unfolding
Durable darkness.

It was the tent and citadel of the many stars
It was the rampart of the loud highway
And we slept there, waking
Into the thunder and silence of the unfolding
Durable journey.

The Plastic Glass

A saint I heard of saw the world
Suspended in a golden globe; so I saw
Shattuck Avenue and the Safeway Stores
In Herndon's globe of friendly credit.

And where the car moved on, there the whole trash
Flats of Berkeley floated in suspense
Gold to the Gate and bellied to the redwood
Cottages.

And I would ask the saint at what expense
This incorporeal vision falls to the lay mind,
And search the breast
For revelations of unquietude.

But in this dear and christian world the blessing
Falls not from above; the grace
Goldens from everyman, his singular credit
In the beatitude of place.

Meeting

Once there lived on the east side of the city
One who wished to meet
One who lived on the west side of the city,
A thousand miles away.

A thousand years went by.

Then the one who lived on the east side of the city
Set out on the main street
And met the one who lived on the west side of the city
Coming that way.

A thousand years.

Miraculous life! that in its brief and mortal
Progress achieved this union of intents,
Inevitability sprung from the improbable,
Volition moving in the paths of chance.

Graham-Paige

Graham-Paige, a car I once rode in,
Carried me out of this world, and I was afraid of that.
Who wouldn't be? You wouldn't be, I see you
Driving across an equal abyss your heart.

At every crossroad
Pause the exporters of their worldly good
Patient as passive
As if they would untravel if they could.

And my antique memory
Sifts me the Graham as if
Every crossroad
Were a crossways cliff.

So that the power at your hand and foot defrayed
Is all my expectation and dismay.
And at every turn you save me.
You slow and save.

Autumnal

We have lost so many leaves
    in loss, loss, loss
Out of the sky,
What shall we do for shelter to live by?

Not roof shelter, but leaf shelter,
    the tentative
Crosswise cover
Which a thousand light ideas give.

Retire under somebody's constructed rafters
    or be grieved that a truthful brain
Exists under a truthful sky
With no palaver between.

Matter of Fact

In the midmost and sensible real of the years of my life
Hallucination like a storm
Comes to its feet beside me
Named by your name and calling me by mine.

So that lamp, storm, student, and friend
As it were love me,
And it is my luck
To love them dearly, as you demand.

They are sensible real as the life of my years
And I love them
As a matter of fact.
And I love you as a fiction of theirs.

Riddle

You are a riddle I would not unravel,
You are the riddle my life comprehends.
And who abstracts the marvel
Abstracts the story to its sorriest ends.

But not your riddle. It is patent,
Never more than it says, and since that is
Impossible, it is the marvel
Nobody, as I am nobody, believes.

Kind

When I think of my kindness which is tentative and quiet
And of yours which is intense and free,
I am in elaboration of knowledge impatient
Of even the patientest immobility.

I think of my kind, which is the human fortune
To live in the world and make war among its friends,
And of my version, which is to be moderately peaceful,
And of your version; and must make amends

By my slow word to your wish which is mobile,
Active and moving in its generous sphere.
This is the natural and the supernatural
Of humankind of which I grow aware.

from "Neighbors & Constellations," *Poems 1930–1960*

The Campaign

My Packard Bell was set up in the vacant lot near the stump
Of the old peach tree. Before it, a love-seat
In tan and green told us what comfort said.
And many looked over us, or sat on the ground, why not?
There certainly were not enough ashtrays for everybody.

And from there it began.
All down the dingle through the mustard ran the voices,
All down the shale in the sunlight ran the faces,
A board fence on the left and a board fence on the right,
Because after all this was private property.

And this is what they said:
He was a child of the people and he will be a man of the people.
He read the Bible at his mother's knee
And that Bible has followed him
All the days of his life.

This is what they said:
The sovereign state of Alabama
Gives you a leader of the people for the people
All the days of his life.
Equal educational opportunity, political opportunity, economic opportunity,
Ability, honesty, integrity, widows and orphans.

Canal Zone deems it a privilege
To second the nomination of that great
All the days of his life.
This is what they said. This is what Cooper Blane
Representing the sovereign state of New Jersey said.

Now all the apples in our apple orchard
Are ripening toward fall
And on our poles the beans are greening fast
The pods with sun alert.

And stubble in the field keeps springing yet
In fresh weed, white puffs of daisy weed,
The cat after the gophers
And the breeze brisk.

Round the ears of Packard Bell brisks the breeze
Blows the volume loud and away,
Puffs of volume pile up in the fence corners
Where the cat is active.

What do we understand?
First of all, we know the speakers are speaking the English language.
We can tell that from our love-seat, and others agree.
Second, they are both loud, lively both, and there are two of them.
Who are you for?

Now enters from the upper left, the hill slope,
A dog. After the cat.
For a while we miss the whole campaign,
But later the dog comes round for friendship.
Pats him the taxpayer and the tax receiver.

Now enters from the upper right a fisherman.
He leans to hear what's sounding on the screen
Then wordlessly he fades
Down the green sidepatch and the cliff steps
To the roaring bay, leaving no vote behind.

Ladies and gentlemen, when I spoke to you last
In Pawtucket, Maine, the tide was coming in
With a long roar against the shingle of the world.

And ladies and gentlemen I say to you
Vote now against corruption, calumny,
Crime, evil, and corruption,
For the tide is coming in
With a long foreign roar against the world.
Against Winthrop Rockefeller, fair play,
Farm money, cartels, bourbon, and the fifth districts of the world.

Slowly comes up the moon over Lottie's rabbit shed,
Fencing into the sky its bars of protest,
But the vote midwest moves at another cycle
Of midnight desperate.

South Dakota five no,
Robert J. Martin of the fifth district, no.
And at the four hundred and eightieth slogan
The yes and the yes that will survive the midnight.

One sure thing is
That the tough tubes on this little old Packard Bell
Jiggling and jumping in the twi- and moonlight,
Hot as hornets in the excitement,
Won't set the beans on fire, and won't
Harm the cat, and won't
Even warm us where we sit and listen,
But will burn away
Lively as bugs in the midsummer
To get the last yes and no in the midsummer
On record to the moon's blanched countenance.
Who are you for?

Mercury

Then have mercy upon me.
Let one who has no care,
Sees not me there,
Likes not if he sees,
And would not, had he care,
Have mercy upon me.

He is my black mercury
Against the world's glass
To which all figures come and pass
Fair as they are in their own loving sight.
He is the black night
Which brings myself to the face of the glass.

In my indelibility
Have mercy upon me,
Quick neutral who does me forget,
Stand not
Fast at the sheer glass of my life
To make my life myself.

Conjure

I was sitting in what that afternoon I thought to be
The vacuum of my life,
Watching the bars of cloud darken over the housetops,
And calling to mind you, as if from far away,
As if by conjure to my lonesome wish,

When lounged in the after-school boy from down the street,
From his own vacuum, "What's new?"
Nothing. What's new with you?
"Well, I'll tell you—" Conjure as ever
Far from the cause summons its consequence.

Sheep

Led by Johns Hopkins on a trip through the heart
To the uttermost reaches of the body,
I was disappointed by X-ray and camera
At what was to be found there.

Mostly I missed the green pastures
Which I knew lay on either side of the path,
The running streams of tears in their salty waters,
Their crystal waters, and the steadfast sheep.

Sheep of my heart, where do you nibble,
At the pump of the ventricle, course of the artery,
That you do not look up into the camera
To tell on what you feed?

Fish

A radioactive fish is one charged
With more of the universe that he can bear,
And in this charge he is familiar.

Through depths of our galaxy, umbrageous swells,
Coral canyons, the fish
Flicker in their schools and perish.

And we in ours flicker and are consumed
Whether or not we eat
Their bread and bait.

By too much universe we taste our diet
Enriched until
One fish, one loaf, one life is bountiful.

Monkey

God, a man at Yale, adopted a monkey
In order to raise him up in his own image,
But only in some respects could the monk identify,
Could learn manners, but not the word of God.

Ah, always it was so, meditated the monkey dazzled and befuddled,
Out of my tree I fell in the forest of Eden,
Or if I mannerly ate, it was the wrong apple,
Or if I climbed I died.

And this is all, I guess, a semantical series
Of my ascent and fall.
His tree is not my tree, His word, my word;
His Yale, my Yale.

The Savages

As we rowed from our ships and set foot on the shore
In the still coves,
We met our images.

Our brazen images emerged from the mirrors of the wood
Like yelling shadows,
So we searched our souls,

And in that hell and pit of everyman
Placed the location of their ruddy shapes.
We must be cruel to ourselves.

Then through the underbrush we cut our hopes
Forest after forest to within
The inner hush where Mississippi flows

And were in ambush at the very source,
Scalped to the cortex. Yet bought them off.
It was an act of love to seek their salvation.

President Jackson asked,
What good man would prefer a forested country ranged with savages
To our extensive republic studded with cities
With all the improvements art can devise or industry execute?

Pastor Smiley inquired,
What good man would allow his sins or his neighbors'
To put on human dress and run in the wilds
To leap out on innocent occasions?

Miss Benedict proposed,
The partial era of enlightenment in which we live
Brings Dionysus to the mesa and the cottonwood grove,

And floats Apollo to the barrows of the civic group
To ratify entreaties and to harp on hope.

Professor Roy Harvey Pearce quoted,
These savages are outlandish Tartars and Cain's children,
Though someone reported once, "They do not withhold assent
From the truth set forth in a credible manner."
Is it possible?

Henry David Thoreau,
The most popular highbrow overseas reading-material
For our armed forces, because while they work and wait
They see before them in the green shade
His ruddy image, said, as his last word when he died, *Indians.*

Reading today this manual of wisdom,
In the still coves
We meet our images

And, in ambush at the very source,
Would buy them off. It is an act of love
To seek their salvation.

One party to the purchase
Receipts the purchase price and hands us back
His token of negotiation which redeems:

We cannibals must help these Christians.

Sisyphus

When Sisyphus was pushing the stone up the mountain,
Always near the top,
As you remember, at the very tip of the height,
It lapsed and fell back upon him,
And he rolled to the bottom of the incline, exhausted.

Then he got up and pushed up the stone again,
First over the grassy rise, then the declivity of dead man's gulch,
Then the outcroppings halfway, at which he took breath,
Looking out over the rosy panorama of Helicon;
Then finally the top

Where the stone wobbled, trembled, and lapsed back upon him,
And he rolled again down the whole incline.
Why?
He said a man's reach must exceed his grasp,
Or what is Hades for?

He said, it's not the goal that matters, but the process
Of reaching it, the breathing joy
Of endeavor, and the labor along the way.
This belief damned him, and damned, what's harder,
The heavy stone.

Oedipus

The gang wanted to give Oedipus Rex a going away present.
He had been a good hard-working father and king.
And besides it is the custom in this country
To give gifts on departure.

But we didn't know what to give Oedipus; he had everything.
Even in his loss, he had more than average.
So we gave him a travelling case, fitted, which we personally
Should have liked to receive.

David

Goliath stood up clear in the assumption of status,
Strong and unquestioning of himself and others,
Fully determined by the limits of his experience.
I have seen such a one among surgeons, sergeants,
Deans, and giants, the power implicit.

Then there was David, who made few assumptions,
Had little experience, but for more was ready,
Testing and trying this pebble or that pebble,
This giant or that giant.
He is not infrequent.

How could Goliath guess, with his many assumptions,
The force of the slung shot of the pure-hearted?
How could David fear, with his few hypotheses,
The power of status which is but two-footed?
So he shot, and shouted!

Speed

A light year is a cell year.
Nothing harries it on but its own speed,
Nothing halts it but its round roll.
It rushes through space as through a lifetime of incarceration.

Unconscionable to me is the speed of a light year
Which I cannot follow with my mind's eye
Or hear rushing and rattling with my heart's ear,
But stands still around me in the perpetual moment of the universe.

In the real year into which I was born,
Autumn succeeds summer and every flower
Lives hastily through the steps of its day
Filled with the clamor of seconds and happenings.

How can I fathom the millenial views
Of sky from cell walls which appertain
To eternity, when here at hand
Gardens of time happen, come into bloom, fade, happen again?

Generation

I saw a work so good,
Strong, delicate, and exact,
It breathed a cool wind
In a breathless day
And set the day in my heart
Like a bronze plaque.

I thought of its maker apt
In his youth to this work,
And I turned to his son to say
Thank you for him, thank him.
But did not, not to bring
To his face that shade.

I saw the sunny round
And restless warmth of the son
In his own energy rapt
To his own will, and learned
How after the father's work
We are Joseph's sons.

When I telephoned a friend, her husband told me
She's not here tonight, she's out saving the Bay.
She is sitting and listening in committee chambers,
Maybe speaking, with her light voice
From the fourteenth row, about where
The birds and fish will go if we fill in the Bay.

The fish, she says, include starry flounder,
Pacific herring, rockfish, surfperches,
And the flat fish who come to the spawning flats
In the shallow waters near the narrow shores.
The shadow-look you know, the fish shooting
In that light green shallow, a dark arrow.

Otherwise we will get a bowling alley,
A car park and golf course, with financing,
Sift up the shallows into a solid base
With sand dredged from the deeper channels, brought in scows
Or hopper dredges, and dumped on the fish, and then paved over
For recreation with no cost to the city.

And so we hear the sides, the margins speaking:
To allow the Commission in the public interest
Permits for the recovery of sand and gravel
From the submerged tidelands of the state,
Fill of unlimited quality, clean sand
Replenished by the southern littoral drift;

Or yet, Dear Sirs: Your bill flies in the face
Of the U.S. Army Engineers' Barrier Study,
The Delta Study, Transportation Study,

Even the Petroleum Institute plan for bringing freighters
And hundreds of workers in to Contra Costa
To boat, bathe, drink, and return these waters.

A student I remember said to me, My mother
Wants me to be a banker, but I want to be
A sanitary engineer, spending all that money
Back toward the sea. Do you think it's possible?
See how these hills shape down back of the college
In summer streaked with little dry arroyos,
In winter running over, rush and freshet,
Through storm drains, cellars, sometimes parlors,
    straight away
Down to the sea. Think of the veins
Of this earth all flowing raining water,
The drove of rivers in the pipes we've laid.

Effluent, said my student, there's a word.
Give me a choice between it and *débris*
And any day I'd choose *effluent.*
Cover and fill is bleach and burn, with tires
Sticking up out of the muck, and loads
Of old brush and tree branches crisping away there.
Not for me, I like the purest water
Sparkling green under a soil, and it can breeze
Out of our pipes and chemicals, lucent as
The rain itself, around the bodies
Of fish and swimmers.

Saving the bay,
Saving the shoals of day,
Saving the tides of shallows deep begun
Between the moon and sun.

Saving the sidings of the Santa Fé.
Saving the egret and the herring run,

Cane and acacia, mallow and yarrow save,
Against the seventh wave,

Boundary and margin, meeting and met,
So that the pure sea will not forget,
Voracious as it is, its foreign kind,
And so the land,

Voracious as it is, will not redeem
Another's diadem.
Saving the shores,
Saving the lines between

Kelp, shrimp, and the scrub green,
Between the lap of waters
And the long
Shoulder of stone.

Therein, between, no homogeneous dredge,
But seedy edge
Of action and of chance
Met to its multiple and variable circumstance.

> Though a news column says that Aquatic Park is a
> police headache,
> In the past year, eighty-seven arrests
> Of characters for crimes better not talked about,
> That the lake is a favorite dumping spot for hot safes,
> Burglary tools, stripped bikes, even a body.
>
> Yet a notice says, Next week at Aquatic Park,
> The V-Drive Boating Club holds its annual race—
> Everybody comes out for this event—
> These are the world's fastest boats, faster than hydros,
> Needing the quiet water the embankment provides.

And a letter from a statistician, fond of the facts,
Compares the use of Aquatic Park to the Rose Garden:
the same pattern;
Fewest people, about five each, on a Friday of terrible
weather,
Next, about fifty, on a warm Wednesday afternoon,
Most, a hundred and fifty, on a clear windy Saturday.
Signed, sincerely, Statistician.

Some live in the deeps, a freighter
Plying between here and Yokohama.
Some live in the rose gardens,
Deeps of a street, a two-storied
Observer and participant, daily
Moving out into the traffic, back into it
Where curtains billow in their breakfast room.
The deeps. Some
Live in the margins. Have they the golden mean?

Freight whistles reach here and the fire engines
Coming from town, foundry hammers
Among the wash of waves.
Kelp drifts them up afloat, and suddenly
They are in the tinder world of lizards.
Cut ashore they bask and breathe
And then plunge back
Down the long glints that take their weight.
At home. At home. But which?

Likely a sea captain will live in a margin
But never wants to, wants a deep molded farm;
Likely an architect, but mainly weekends.
On the weekdays, along the Bay margin
Little happens, small objects
Breed and forage. Flights come in and vanish.
Solicitudes entail solicitudes.

Dredge the channel, reinforce the sea wall
And we shall have deep calling to deep directly.

She starts to speak, my friend in her light voice,
Of margins: marshes, birds, and embarcaderos.
Truths spread to dry like nets, mended like nets,
Draw in at the edges their corruptions,
To let the moving world of bay and town
Mingle, as they were amphibian again.

Saving the bay. Saving the blasted bay.
That there be margins of the difference,
Scrap heap and mobile, wind ridge and ledge,
Mud and débris. That there be
Shore and sea.

Love at a distance can mean
Love of a dozen
Students sitting around for the last time
Before summer, to come no more,
Tired and sore,
Yet to be loved in their measureless aptitude.

Love at a distance can be the good
Work done by a workman, so simplified
He could not do better if he tried;
So austere, thank or praise
Only by use.
Or can be the distance at which you measureless move.

That is, far off.
So that love can be drawn
In filaments of thought, in lines as thin
As the lines latitudes rest upon.
From plenty, from perfection, marking these
Measureless distances.

After I come home from the meeting with friends
I lie to sleep on the turn of the earth as it spins
Toward the sun, toward the rising light as the day begins
And think of those I love as the day ends.

They are clearing the dishes, sweeping the ashes away,
They are threading the traffic, moving toward distances,
Disposing their hearts as the dark midnight spins,
Gathering toward the light of the new day.

Spent and regained, their strength for a cause, for a plain
Defeat or delight, strengthens my heart as it moves
Into sleep, and my sleep as it runs in the grooves
Toward the east where a waking heart is more than mine.

The doctor who sits at the bedside of a rat
Obtains real answers—a paw twitch,
An ear tremor, a gain or loss of weight,
No problem as to which
Is temper and which is true.
What a rat feels, he will do.

Concomitantly then, the doctor who sits
At the bedside of a rat
Asks real questions, as befits
The place, like where did that potassium go, not what
Do you think of Willie Mays or the weather?
So rat and doctor may converse together.

The entrepreneur chicken shed his tail feathers, surplus
Fat, his comb, wing weight, down to a mere
Shadow, like a Graves bird ready to sing.
For him every morning
Paradise Merchant Mart reopened its doors
With regular fire sales, Shoe Parlor
Blackened its aroma, Professional
Building ran its elevators up and down
So fast that pulled teeth turned up in other mouths.

Activity. The tax base broadened in the sunlight
As gradually sun spreads wider after coffee.
It was a busy world on that side of the road,
For which the entrepreneur chicken was in his able
Way responsible.
At noon, loans, mortgages, personal interest,
At night notarized after-images, as if by sundown
The elevator had turned to moving sidewise
Frames and phrases to be read and reread.

He was not boss or mayor, but he certainly was
Right on that spinning wheel which spun the public
In and out of his stores, and his pleasantries
Began to spin the flesh right off his bones.
That is why the chicken began to sing
High, not loud, and why transparencies
Of pipestems were his legs, his beak aloft,
His feathers lean, drawing the busy air,
And why he crossed the road.

Daniel Boone stepped up to a window
(What! a window?) with his trusty rifle,
And he shot his bear.
This was some bear.
It was a millionaire,
A Harvard, London, and a South Sea bear
A French, a football bear.

A corporate family
And incorporate party,
Thoroughly transistized
Into his rocking chair,
Built and bureaucratized,
Daddied and deared and dared,
Indomitable bear.

What an investment
Of time, of love too,
All in one body,
A computation
Of maximal purpose,
A one-man world.

Daniel is angry
That after the eighth grade
This bear should travel
So far ahead.
Unfair
That a bear
Should rock so big a chair.

So gets him, and as he is got
Shows him
Shows us
It takes no complicated bomb or plot
To win again us back to wilderness,
But just one pot, pure, individual, shot.

As difference blends into identity
Or blurs into obliteration, we give
To zero our position at the center,
Withdraw our belief and baggage.

As rhyme at the walls lapses, at frontiers
Customs scatter like a flight of snow,
And boundaries moonlike draw us out, our opponents
Join us, we are their refuge.

As barriers between us melt, I may treat you
Unkindly as myself, I may forget
Your name as my own. Then enters
Our anonymous assailant.

As assonance by impulse burgeons
And that quaver shakes us by which we are spent,
We may move to consume another with us,
Stir into parity another's cyphers.

Then when our sniper steps to a window
In the brain, starts shooting, and we fall surprised,
Of what we know not do we seek forgiveness
From ourselves, for ourselves?

In the town where every man is king,
Every man has one subject,
Every man bends to his own foot.
Bring on the mirror that he may properly bend.
But who will bring it on?

In the castle where is no hunger and no need,
Every man gives gifts and receives
Gifts. But of these only his own
Enhance him, the ring giver.
He must wear his ring.

Gradually, as he resolves the oppression of his edicts,
Losing his fellow lords to dim perspectives,
Monoliths of rock and stone, even
Of reinforced concrete, become before him
Mirrors. He licks the glass.

I walked along the river path, the river
    I never lived beside,
    And met there, hook and line, king of that kingdom
    I would not recognize.

    He was the golden branch of Eliot, of
    Those wasteland parties where I had to play
    Tiresias, and he was a king
    Whom I did not believe.

    Laius nor any man's killed by his son
    Unless he wills it, so I said
    To this old bird where he sat, Why let come riding
    The handsomest of your brood to do you in?

    And he wept, Because it is him or me—
    Should he not survive me, he survives not
    All that I was: alcoholic
    At forty, cheat at forty-five,
    Coward at fifty, these he will be

    Over again in sequence, while I sit
    Mourning myself in him. Tell him to hurry.
    That was the waste land as it dawned upon me
    To see it was my friend sat by the river
    Crouching and fishing in his father's form.

Throwing his life away,
He picks at and smells it.
Done up. When did I do this up?
I date its death to the time someone
Said something.
Back then.
Everything else, all striving, making,
Marrying, error,
Is this old bird.
Pah! He throws it.
As the long string lengthens
Out of his hand,
It begins unwinding
The ligaments of his hand.

Still early morning, the wind's edge
Catches in veins the edges that stick in them;
Thorny friends, burrs of confusion,
Pressures of office that take a rhomboid wrench
Through every breath. I would, I say,
To the genii that live in the long lamp of hope,
Have them all rounded, is that not possible?

All edges rounded till they will bubble
Easily together? Slowly the sun,
Rising up over the roofs and trees,
Brings another way beyond my wish.
The edges meet and fit, the angles turn
To complement, merge and sparkle, vein to vein,
As the sharp morning seeks delineation.

Grievances: the warm fogs of summer
Preserve them on the bough; finally a chill
Reason sends them flying off and away.

I keep one or two and press them in a book,
And when I show them to you they have crumbled
To powder on the page. So I rehearse.

But I do not believe. I believe rather,
The stems of grievance put down their heavy roots
And by the end of summer crack the pavement.

When the sun came, the rooster expanded to meet it,
Stood up, stirred his wings,
Raised his red comb and sentence
Rendered imperative utterance
Saying, Awake. Nothing answered.
He took in a beakful of air; yes, first it was he,
And engendered a number of hard-shelled cacklers,
One for each day in the week.
They grew in their yard, the dust in their feathers,
Who heard them praise him? An egg.

In the night, in the barn, the eggs wakened and cried,
Saying, We have been wakened,
And cried, saying Father, so named him,
His feathers and beak from the white and the yolk.
Father, who newly can ring out the welkin,
And crow, we will listen to hear.
As toward him we move, and the wings of our feathers grow
bright,
And we spring from the dust into flame
He will call us his chickens.
But that was already their name.

Does the world look like a park to you? Yes, almost suddenly
The world looks like a park.
Are there worn spots in the shorn grass? Yes, under
The childrens' feet,
And under the feet of bison behind trees.

Are there temperature controls in the park? Yes, the warm sun
Is made shady, and the warm shade
Sunny. Feelings too,
Whether out on the shorn lawns or behind the bushes,
Run hot and cold to the edges of Africa and Chicago.

It is a national park, then? Yes, national
In its red, white, and blue bunting, in its scope and convenience.
Hear the bears groping for sliced bacon.
In the national parks, however, the turbulence
Still perseveres, of waters?

Glaciers and gorges move down to the warm lawns?
Yes, but just to the point where the dams take them. Then they
ripple
Over the flooded farms of the Havasupai,
Of Nefertiti and Osiris,
And carry them softly off to the park's museums.

Every day when she came to the steps that led
　　To the class to be taught,
　　The bells in the tower were telling the cost of the hour,
　　And there they met.
　　They were ready and she was ready.

　　One day, by a lost minute or so, she came
　　To the silent spot
　　Where she waited the bells to ring and they did not,
　　The future fallen bells, but had flown
　　Into a past over and done.

　　Where had the unsounded hour gone?
　　It was ready and she was ready.

In the neighborhood of my childhood, a hundred lungers
Coughed in their tents like coyotes.
The sand was dry and saged with mesquite.
Even so, from mountains the dew dropped
Down on the canvas in the early dark.
The kerosene puffed away as I fell to sleep.

In that rich landscape I was deprived,
Because no negro coughed among the tents, moved
Outward among the distant orange groves.
A square shot of Indians walked the coals,
But so pure the absence of black skin, I thought
All the sorrows of the world were white.

Later, a stonewall neighbor Harriman's
Krazy Kat neither spoke to us, nor spoke
To any negro neighbor because we had none.
Mexican squatters in the boxes in the dry river
Sent no drift of blackness to our dream.
Black Sambo was our child.

When land gave no relief, across the plains
The white and blistered figures in jalopies
Moved into town, but did not come to college.
And so who were they? Such an array
In sandy paleness needed to be brown.
Minority, myself.

Deprived.
Out of the sunny and the shadowy scenes
Where I look back with wonderment and love,
An oversimple marginal deployment
Of absence,
A relentless letting be.

Down from another planet they have settled to mend
    The Hampton Institute banisters. They wear bow ties and braces.
    The flutings they polish with a polished hand.

    Wingless, they build and repair
    The mansions of what we have thought to be our inheritance.
    Caution and candor they labor to maintain.

    They are out of phase. I prepare
    To burn all gentle structures, greek or thatch,
    Under the masterful torch of my president here and abroad,

    Till stubble outsmolders, and muslim and buddhist crack
    In the orbit of kiln.
                                        A smoke
    To some calm Christian planet will drift,

    To where they are mending their mansions, beside of whose doors
    They are standing at ease, they are lifting the fans
    Of unburdenable wings.

When I was eight, I put in the left-hand drawer
Of my new bureau a prune pit.
My plan was that darkness and silence
Would grow it into a young tree full of blossoms.

Quietly and unexpectedly I opened the drawer a crack
And looked for the sprouts; always the pit
Anticipated my glance, and withheld
The signs I looked for.

After a long time, a week, I felt sorry
For the lone pit, self-withheld,
So saved more, and lined them up like an orchard.
A small potential orchard of free flowers.

Here memory and storage lingered
Under my fingerprints past retrieval,
Musty and impatient as a prairie
Without its bee.

Some friends think of this recollection
As autobiography. Others think it
A plausible parable of computer analysis.
O small and flowering orchard of free friends!

Have I outgrown you?
Have we lived in a little city together
And now while you map your local entertainments
Do I go out upon some new portage,
Desperate to be lonelier and beyond,
Wealthier to ascend?

You write that things are going well in town and I see them
Going well. But by what luminant?
Bobby, see Jane jump; Eve, Adam. Clearly
Temptation brings the light so full to bear
That you and semblance have the same substance.
Am I going away to your nearest distance?

Apart from branches in courtyards and small stones,
The countryside is beyond me.
I can go along University Avenue from Rochester to Sobrante
And then the Avenue continues to the Bay.

Often I think of the dry scope of foothill country,
Moraga Hill, Andreas, Indian country, where I was born
And where in the scrub the air tells me
How to be born again.

Often I think of the long rollers
Breaking against the beaches
All the way down the coast to the border
On bookish cressets and culverts blue and Mediterranean.

There I break
In drops of spray as fine as letters
Blown high, never to be answered,
But waking am the shore they break upon.

Both the dry talkers, those old Indians,
And the dry trollers, those old pirates,
Say something, but it's mostly louder talking,
Gavel rapping, and procedural dismays.

Still where we are, and where we call and call,
The long rollers of the sea come in
As if they lived here. The dry Santa Ana
Sweeps up the town and takes it for a feast.

Then Rochester to El Sobrante is a distance
No longer then my name.

PS 3525 .I4835 T6
Miles, Josephine, 1911-
To all appearances